Also by Melanie Bockmann:

Just Plane Crazy

To order, call **1-800-765-6955**.

Visit us at www.reviewandherald.com for information on other Review and Herald® products.

THE MYERS BROTHERS FLIP FROM FAME TO GLORY

UnRapped

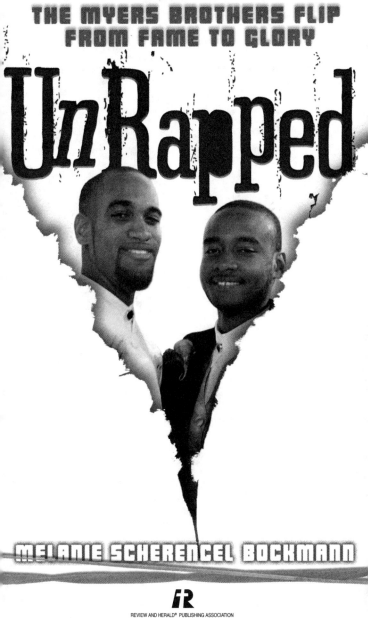

MELANIE SCHERENCEL BOCKMANN

REVIEW AND HERALD® PUBLISHING ASSOCIATION
Since 1861 | www.reviewandherald.com

Published by Review and Herald® Publishing Association, Hagerstown, MD
21741-1119

Texts credited to NIV are from the *Holy Bible, New International Version.*
Copyright © 1973, 1978, 1984, International Bible Society. Used by permission
of Zondervan Bible Publishers.

Review and Herald® titles may be purchased in bulk for educational, business,
fund-raising, or sales promotional use. For information, please e-mail
SpecialMarkets@reviewandherald.com.

The Review and Herald® Publishing Association publishes biblically-based materi-
als for spiritual, physical, and mental growth and Christian discipleship.

The author assumes full responsibility for the accuracy of all facts and quotations as
cited in this book.

This book was
Edited by Penny Estes Wheeler
Cover design by Ron J. Pride
Interior design by Heather Rogers
Typeset: Bembo 11/13

PRINTED IN U.S.A.

11   10   09   08   07   5   4   3   2   1

Library of Congress Cataloging-in-Publication Data

Bockmann, Melanie, 1974-
  UnRapped : the Myers brothers flip from fame to glory / Melanie Bockmann.
    p. cm.
  1. Myers, Sean. 2. Myers, Ivor. 3. Christian biography. 4. Musicians—
Biography. 5. Clergy—Biography. 6. Boogie Monsters (Musical group) I. Title.
BR1700.3.B63 2007
277.3'0830922—dc22
  [B]

                                2007025025

ISBN 978-0-8280-2073-2

CHAPTER 1

It was over.

The music, the money, the fame—all of it. Even though only a few months had passed since they walked away from the music industry the experience seemed like a distant memory, a whole different lifetime. Sean leaned against the kitchen counter in his parents' house and sipped a glass of water. He shook his head in amazement as he watched his brother Ivor eat breakfast. He was wearing a Target store uniform. Target! Ivor looked like a different person without his dreadlocks, baggy pants, and expensive jewelry.

"Man, I think you're probably the most famous employee Target has ever had," Sean teased.

Ivor seemed carefree as he swallowed the last bite of his cereal and pushed away from the table. "At least when people ask why I'm working in a store instead of rapping with the Boogiemonsters, I can explain it to them. Unlike you, out there on the street flagging traffic, and people wonder what in the world you're doing there. All *you* can do is wave."

"Yeah, you should see the looks on people's faces when they recognize me!" Sean laughed, and then grew serious. "But you know, I wouldn't change a thing. How this all turned out, I mean. It was supposed to be this way. God brought us here."

"I know." Ivor rinsed his cereal bowl in the sink and dried his hands on a towel. "It's weird, because I'm happy. I'm wearing a Target vest, getting ready to go to a job where I make hardly any money—and I'm happy."

The brothers looked at each other, saying nothing. Their experiences had bonded them in such a way that sometimes they could say more in silence than they could with words.

The stairs creaked and their friend Tammy, who was visiting from Jamaica, came around the corner into the kitchen. "Hey, do you guys know a rapper named Biggie Smalls?" she asked as she opened the refrigerator and bent down for a look inside.

"Notorious B.I.G.? Of course we know him. Everybody does," Ivor replied. "We grew up in the same neighborhood he did."

"Yeah, and we were touring with him only a few months ago," Sean added. "Why do you ask?"

Tammy paused and looked back at them. "Because he's dead," she said quietly.

Sean felt his chest tighten. "What do you mean he's dead?"

"He was murdered last night," Tammy continued. "After the Soul Train Awards in Los Angeles. It's on TV now—go see for yourselves."

Sean and Ivor ran to the living room. Sure enough, with Biggie Smalls' picture filling the screen, the story unfolded on the national news as the brothers watched in disbelief.

According to the news report, Biggie Smalls and his entourage of friends and bodyguards left the

Soul Train Awards party at 12:45 a.m. to return to their hotel. While they waited at a traffic light only 50 yards away from where the party was held, a Chevy Impala pulled up beside them. The driver of the Impala rolled down his window and shot several rounds of his 9 mm blue steel pistol into the Suburban that carried Biggie and his friends. Four of the bullets took a destructive path through Biggie Smalls' chest, and minutes later a doctor at Cedars-Sinai Medical Center pronounced him DOA, dead on arrival. Though assumptions were already circulating that it was a retaliation killing involving a feud between rivaling East coast and West coast rappers, the murderer was still at large.

Sean stared at the television while Ivor swallowed hard and wordlessly sank into the couch. Two years before Biggie Smalls' career had been propelled into further success with the debut of his solo album, "Ready to Die."

Now as the details of his death emerged, that album title seemed eerily prophetic.

Through the shock that tingled in his mind, Sean could hear an inner voice reminding him that he, his brother Ivor, and Biggie Smalls had all been called out of the music industry. The only difference was he and Ivor had been called out by Life. Biggie had been called out by Death.

A flood of questions surged through Sean's mind, all starting with the words "what if." What if they had still been involved in the dangerous playground of the rap music industry? What if they had attended the Soul Train Awards party the night before? What if their fame had eventually cost them what it had cost Biggie Smalls?

Sean pressed the "off" button on the remote control and the TV went silent. His mind raced back to the beginning, back to when the mesmerizing allure of success in the entertainment industry whispered an invitation to him. He and three others had answered that call and entered a surreal world of money, fame, girls, possessions, and power. Now, on the other side, he could see it all as it truly was. It had been a strange, incredible journey.

★ ★ ★

"Shhh! Don't make a sound!"

Sean's mom held his 4-year-old body close to her and peered with wide eyes into the foreboding darkness. The movement of the curtains in the night breeze cast slippery shadows across her face, and Sean could feel the rapid pounding of her heart against his cheek. He looked down at his older brothers, Ivor and Rhoan, crouched and flattened against the wall right under the window. How he wished his dad was home to help protect them. Just outside, hiding in the bushes, were rough-faced men with guns, and Sean knew that at any moment their plans to assault the frightened family would be put into action.

Sean's dad, a high-ranking military officer in the Jamaican Special Forces and covert counterintelligence unit, had developed a formidable reputation among the drug lords in Jamaica after leading raids that helped to sabotage local drug activity. This weekend Sean's dad was out of town, and the drug lords were about to have their revenge.

"What are we going to do?" Rhoan whispered, but his mother shook her head. *Not a word*, her motion commanded. *Not a sound.*

A moment later light from the next-door neighbor's home flooded the yard, and the sound of rapid gunshots rang out. Sean's body tensed with each exploding bullet, and he covered his ears against the deafening reports. Then the last shot echoed into the night and was swallowed by silence.

The family hovered by the window until they heard the familiar sound of their neighbor's voice calling to them. The men with guns were gone, and Sean's mom reluctantly led the boys out of their hiding place. Their neighbor had seen the men lurking in the bushes, and had scared them away by turning on the blinding lights and firing his gun.

A couple of days later Sean's father returned home. From his bedroom Sean could hear his parents discussing the dangerous situation the family had encountered and the looming threat of a future assault.

"Those men will not give up this easily," Sean heard his father say grimly. "They will be back to take their revenge against me. And what then? We may not be so fortunate next time. I will not have my family endangered this way."

"But what can we do?" his mother asked. "Where can we go?"

"I'm going to do something," his father said. "I'll find a way."

Determined to protect his family, Sean's father

made rapid plans to move his wife and sons far away from the island life they knew in Jamaica, to a place where they would be out of reach of the drug lords' revenge. Several months later, Sean and his brother Ivor found themselves living with their parents in a new and fascinating place in America called Brooklyn, New York. It was a turning point on a course charted for them by an unseen hand.

CHAPTER 2

The door slammed behind Sean and Ivor as they burst into the house, breathless. Both boys dropped their school books into precarious stacks on the floor and kicked off their shoes. Although several years had passed since they first arrived in the United States with their parents, adjusting to a new culture had not been easy, and the boys still felt like outsiders most of the time. "I'm sick of it," Ivor said, plopping down on the sofa and crossing his arms. "I just want to fight back and teach them to leave me alone once and for all."

Sean sighed and wedged his chin between his two hands as he sat cross-legged on the carpet. He understood how his brother felt. Middle school was hard enough to survive as an average kid, but Sean and Ivor found themselves with an extra challenge—a strong Jamaican accent that often made them the center of jokes not only with their fellow students, but also with some of the teachers. The fact that they had few friends also made them an easy target for gangs of bullies looking for victims with lunch money. Sometimes Sean wondered if they'd ever survive, much less fit in. But they knew better than to complain to their dad about being pushed around. They understood from experience that he would expect them to defend themselves.

"What can we do?" Sean wondered out loud as he thought about the kids with rocks in their hands who had chased them home from school. Sean had imaginary scenarios of revenge that he sometimes played in his head. But in reality, his problems were always still waiting for him just outside his imagination, and he wished there were some way out.

Sean and Ivor's dilemma was the subject of conversation the next time their Uncle Tony came to visit. Uncle Tony was a martial arts instructor who had trained in the art of Wing Chun with a classmate of Bruce Lee, the movie actor famous for his martial arts skills.

"Do you think you could help us, Uncle Tony?" Sean begged. "Just teach us some moves we can use to defend ourselves from the guys who keep picking on us."

Uncle Tony looked at them thoughtfully. "Martial arts training requires a lot of practice and self-discipline," he told them. "Developing the necessary skills takes time. It won't happen overnight."

"We'll practice," Ivor promised for both of them, and the boys looked at their uncle with pleading faces.

"All right," Uncle Tony agreed. "I'll teach you to do a Chi Sao drill. Face each other, and put your forearms against your brother's forearms."

The boys stood in the stance Uncle Tony had described.

"This is important," Uncle Tony continued. "It will help you develop awareness so you can sense and anticipate the reflexes of your opponent. It will also help you learn to counter your opponent's moves quickly."

The boys tried to follow Uncle Tony's instructions as closely as possible. Their fascination grew as Uncle Tony explained the fundamental principles of body movement and gave them turning, stepping, and punching drills to practice on their own.

Between visits from Uncle Tony, Sean and Ivor rehearsed their drills until they could execute each move smoothly and precisely. And as their martial arts skills increased, so did their confidence.

"I'm not afraid of anybody anymore!" Ivor told Sean one day. Ivor was admiring the Chinese throwing stars that were the latest addition to his martial arts weapon collection. "I don't care who comes after me, they'll wish they hadn't. Remember that bully, Rob? He actually ran from me the other day."

"I'm not afraid anymore either," Sean confidently agreed. In addition to his martial arts practices, Sean had also taken up gymnastics, and the combination of the two forms of exercise made him quick and agile. And like Ivor, Sean had started an impressive collection of martial arts weaponry.

"I know. You've been developing a little reputation for yourself." Ivor smiled. "I heard that at school the other day you knocked somebody's glasses off with a reversed roundhouse kick."

"We were just playing around," Sean shrugged.

"Yeah, but the rumor is that everybody had better watch out for you if you're ever not just playing around."

Sean grinned. He couldn't wait to tell Uncle

UnRapped

Tony about his new reputation and his new friends. But the next time he came to visit, Uncle Tony had something besides martial arts on his mind.

"Boys," Uncle Tony said. "I've just made an interesting discovery."

"What's that, Uncle Tony?" Sean asked.

"Well," Uncle Tony continued, "I've been reading my Bible, and everything I can find tells me that the Sabbath is on the seventh day of the week. That's Saturday."

Sean felt curious. His family didn't attend church, but many of his friends did, and everyone knew that the Sabbath was on Sunday. "Are you sure?" Sean asked him.

"Positive," Uncle Tony said. "It's not just in one place, either. It's all through the Bible. Saturday is the day God says is holy."

Ivor seemed curious as well. "What are you going to do about it?"

Uncle Tony looked serious. "Well, now that it has been revealed to me, I'm going to have to start keeping Sabbath on the seventh day—Saturday."

"That blows my mind," Ivor said to Sean later. "Remember the Bible Aunt Polly gave me for my birthday when we first came to America?"

Sean nodded.

"Well," Ivor continued, "I remember holding it and thinking to myself that there was power inside the pages of that book. Like this feeling of awe came over me or something."

Ivor didn't say anything else about Uncle Tony's discovery after that, but Sean became more curious than he ever had been about the Bible. If Saturday was really the Sabbath, and almost everyone was keeping Sunday, what else was in the Bible that they didn't know about? Could it be that there were more discoveries to be made?

It wasn't long, however, before Sean and Ivor forgot all about Uncle Tony's conclusion on the Sabbath. They didn't know that the bit of information Uncle Tony had shared with them would come up again someday in an entirely unexpected place.

CHAPTER 3

As Sean became more involved and skilled in martial arts, he felt himself strangely drawn to the dragons and other symbols of the art of warfare. He developed a fascination with monsters and was deeply entranced by the dark world of evil characters he found in books he read at the library.

"What is that you're reading?" Sean's father asked one day when he noticed his son's imagination being consumed by a book. When he saw the images of strange creatures from the underworld in the book Sean was reading, he was not impressed.

"Get rid of that book," his father demanded. "Sean, if I catch you reading those books again, I'm going to give you the belt. If you're going to read, read something sensible."

Though the threat of punishment loomed over his head, Sean's curiosity about evil beasts and monsters caused him to pursue his addiction in secret. When no one was looking he soaked up the dark stories like a thirsty sponge. Even after his father caught him reading the forbidden books again and followed through with his threat of punishment, Sean was undeterred.

One night Sean and Ivor settled onto the couch

with a bowl of hot, buttered popcorn to watch a movie.

"Are you sure you want to watch this?" Ivor teased as he switched off the lamp. "It's supposed to be really scary."

"Me? Scared? Yeah, right." Sean made a face at his brother and scooped up a handful of popcorn as the theme music began to play and movie images appeared on the screen.

Sean and Ivor watched in the dim light of the television as a bone-chilling horror story unfolded before them. The movie was about Damien, a boy who discovers that he is the antichrist. He is led by a guardian demon to read Revelation 13 in the Bible, where he learns about the mark of the beast and the strange number 666. Damien discovers that the number 666 is on his head underneath his hair, and after that, anyone who discovers his true identity mysteriously dies. When the movie ended, both boys went upstairs to their room.

"Scared?" Ivor asked with a smirk as he flipped the light switch off and crawled into bed.

"No," Sean lied. He climbed into his own bed and pulled the covers up under his nose. Vivid images from the movie kept his imagination awake, and Sean lay in his bed without making a sound. Once again, thoughts about the Bible aroused his curiosity. *Was there really a mark of the beast? What was the significance of the mysterious number 666?* He decided that someday he would read Revelation 13 for himself to try to find the answers.

"You know, the number 666 really is in the

Bible," Sean and Ivor's cousin Susan said in a low voice one day while the three of them were home alone. Susan was visiting from England for the summer. A couple of years older than Sean and Ivor, she seemed to have a knowledgeable air about her, especially since she'd read the book of Revelation in the Bible. As they talked, somehow the subject of the mark of the beast and the number 666 had come up, and Susan held the boys in suspense with her ominous words. "Plus," she continued in deep, serious tones, "there are companies that work for the devil that produce dishwashing liquids and laundry detergents. In fact, you can tell which ones do because if you look on the soapbox, you'll find the mark of the beast printed there."

"What is it?" Ivor asked.

Sean felt a burning surge of panic in his chest, and he looked at Ivor and Susan with wide eyes, not sure if he wanted to know the answer to Ivor's question. Even Ivor seemed to tremble in nervous anticipation, and he looked as if he wished he had not asked.

Susan took a deep breath. "Well," she slowly, "it's a picture of a half moon with a man's face in it." She paused while her words had their effect on her younger cousins. "Do you have a soapbox in the house?" she asked.

"Yes," Ivor answered reluctantly. "We do. Downstairs in the laundry room."

"Let's go!" Susan's challenge hung in the air for a moment while Sean and Ivor looked at each other in terror. Sean's heart pounded as he remembered the movie they'd seen, and he knew Ivor was thinking about the same thing.

Slowly Susan began walking down the stairs to the dark laundry room below. It seemed to the boys that her slow, heavy tread beat a message of doom. But Ivor crept down the steps after her, and Sean followed, trying to swallow a dry lump of dread in his throat. Susan found the box of laundry detergent and picked it up to examine. The boys held their breath while she scanned the front of the box, then the back, then the side. Suddenly she stopped.

"There it is!" Susan whispered, pointing.

It was too much for the boys. Sean and Ivor didn't bother to look at the box. They both ran back up the stairs screaming and tripping over each other until they stood out in the yard in their pajamas, well out of reach of the "evil" laundry detergent.

Later, after the rush of adrenalin had subsided, Sean was able to calm down enough to realize that the mark of the beast couldn't possibly be a symbol on a box of laundry soap. It didn't make sense. But this realization only fueled his curiosity to find out the truth. What *was* the mark of the beast? Was it something he could avoid? Was it something he had already, and just didn't know it?

★ ★ ★

"Hey, what do you think of my vampire teeth?" Sean grinned at Ivor, revealing a jagged row of teeth complete with sharp yellow fangs.

UnRapped

Summer was over, the weather had grown cool, and Halloween had arrived. Sean and Ivor looked forward to trick-or-treating with their friends, and had used costumes to morph themselves into almost unrecognizable creatures. For Sean, it was a chance to be one of the monsters from the stories that still intrigued him.

"Pretty terrifying," Ivor answered, unfazed.

Sean took Ivor's statement as a compliment and admired his grotesque appearance in the mirror one last time before they left the house. By the time Sean and Ivor set out on their bicycles to meet their friends, the pale evening light had evaporated into darkness and streetlights blinked on above them. It was only a short trip along the shadowed sidewalks to where their friends waited. The air buzzed with energy as the group of guys rode around town together, joking and laughing, and playing tricks on each other. They'd stopped on the street corner of a popular neighborhood to plan their trick-or-treating strategy when a car pulled up to the curb, and the window slowly rolled down.

"Sean and Ivor, get into the car!" their dad called.

Sean bent down to look in the car window. "Dad? Is that you?" he asked, surprised to hear his father's voice.

"How did he even find us?" Ivor muttered to Sean under his breath. "He must have been looking for a while."

"Get in the car," Sean's dad repeated more sternly. "You're not going trick or treating."

Confused, Sean and Ivor managed to fit their bicycles in the trunk of the car and then slid into the backseat while their dumbfounded friends stood next to the street and watched.

"Dad, why can't we go trick-or-treating?" Sean asked carefully as he clicked his seatbelt into place.

Dad looked into the rearview mirror as the car pulled away from the curb. "Because it's the devil's holiday!"

"The *what?*" Sean whispered to himself, his mind now thoroughly confounded. His dad was not a religious person, and had never talked about the devil before, but Sean knew better than to argue with him. He silently rode next to Ivor until the car pulled up beside Aunt Carmen's church.

"Oh, I know what happened. Aunt Carmen must have talked to him," Ivor whispered to Sean. "That's probably why all of a sudden he's concerned about the devil and the devil's holiday."

The car stopped and their dad turned around to face the boys. "They're showing a movie here at your Aunt Carmen's church tonight, so this is where you are going to be instead of trick-or-treating."

Sean could feel his brother's anger as they got out of the car. Their father drove away, and Sean and Ivor dragged themselves toward the entrance of the church building. Sean felt angry, too. Instead of having fun trick-or-treating with their friends, they were stuck sitting on a church pew watching a stupid movie. Their father was acting very strangely, and it was interfering with their social life in a big way! Sean sat down on the bench with a defiant thud, thoroughly prepared to be bored out of his mind.

The lights dimmed, and the movie began. Sean tried not to think about the fun his friends were having, or the candy they would be bringing home from their adventures. He looked at Ivor, who sat with his arms crossed and a sullen look on his face. Sean sighed and turned his attention to the screen.

The movie was about a preacher who was determined to teach the gang members in New York City about Jesus Christ. These gang members were caught up in their fights and drugs and sex, and weren't remotely interested in knowing anything about Jesus. In fact, they even threatened the preacher's life. But the preacher wouldn't leave, and as the movie progressed, all of that hatred and anger that motivated the lifestyle of the gang culture began to change, especially with one particular gang member named Nicky Cruz.

Strangely, as he watched the movie, Sean's anger began to subside, replaced with a spirit of peace. He sneaked a glance at Ivor, and it seemed the movie was having a calming effect on him as well. His arms were uncrossed, and the hard look of anger on his face had softened now that he was engrossed in the movie. He was taking in the story through wide eyes, and Sean sensed that the movie was touching him deeply, too.

What is it about Jesus? Sean wondered. *What is it about Jesus that would make a tough gang member put down his weapons, and makes people like that crazy preacher risk their lives to talk about Him?*

When the movie ended, Sean and Ivor waited

for their eyes to adjust to the light, and then stood to leave. "That wasn't so bad, eh?" Sean said with a yawn, stretching his arms. "I thought it was actually pretty interesting."

"Yeah." Ivor looked thoughtful. "I think that was the first time I ever heard anybody really talk about Jesus—you know, besides just hearing His name in swearing, and stuff like that. I wouldn't mind hearing more."

Sean nodded in agreement.

But the days passed and neither of them talked more about the night's events. As the weeks passed, the movie's effect on them gradually faded, and they nearly forgot about it altogether.

CHAPTER 4

Sean could hear the low thump of the music while they were still a couple of blocks away. Drawn to the rhythmic sound, he and Ivor navigated their bicycles down the street past a vacant lot littered with trash. They wound their way through a motley group of people who stood under the awning of a little corner store, watching the boys with curious eyes while sipping cold sodas in the afternoon heat. The sound of the boys' whirring bicycle tires deflected off the intermittent slats of fencing, alternately louder, then softer. Sean squinted against the sun to see an older woman pinning her laundry on a line that stretched from the second-story window. He turned his handlebars to follow Ivor across the street. Nearby, squealing, giggling children ran splashing through water that gushed from the open mouth of a red fire hydrant.

The music grew louder as they turned the corner. Sean had seen them before—older teenagers dancing to the beat of hip-hop music using flattened cardboard boxes on sun-scorched sidewalks—and something about the way the music seemed to flow through their bodies made Sean want to learn how to dance that way himself. Sean and Ivor slowed their bikes to a stop and leaned against a graffiti-covered wall to watch the display from a distance. The body movements of the dancers were fascinating, almost liquid, as they rendered their own interpretation of the music through motion. The black and gray speakers on the boom boxes pulsed and breathed the mesmerizing hip-hop bass line with such intensity that Sean could feel it at the core of his being.

The weeks passed. Each time they saw an impressive new move, Sean and Ivor went home and imitated it in the mirror wearing their hoods and windbreakers—the style of the hip-hop/rap culture. Over and over they practiced until they could break dance and "pop" with the same fluid motion they saw performed on the streets. As with martial arts and gymnastics, a perfect American accent was unnecessary when it came to dancing. No words were needed, because the movement of dance communicated their expression.

"You should see the way they dance in the clubs," Sean's older brother, Rhoan, said one day as he watched the boys practice. "They really know how to move."

Rhoan often took the train through Queens and Brooklyn to uptown Manhattan to go to the club Roxy located in the Bronx, and Sean was so envious he could almost taste it. More than anything, Sean wanted to be old enough to explore the club scene for himself. While he waited impatiently to grow up, he had to rely on Rhoan's descriptions of Manhattan nightlife.

"Tell me! Tell me!" Sean begged. He flopped

down on the floor and looked up at Rhoan expectantly.

"Well, I was in the club, and I saw a man spinning on his back."

"What do you mean?" Sean persisted.

"Let me show you." Rhoan grabbed Sean's leg and spun him around on the floor.

Something clicked in Sean's head. "I can use my own leg as a propeller and make my body spin," he realized out loud.

Before long, Sean and Ivor added the spinning move to their ever-growing repertoire of dance moves. Every free moment they had found them practicing with strong-willed determination to improve their skill.

"I'll bet we could do all of these moves even better," Sean said one day while he and Ivor looked in the garage for boxes to flatten.

"Better?" Ivor sounded intrigued. "How?"

"Well," Sean continued, "I've been thinking. What if we took those same dance techniques we've been learning, and added some aerial moves from our martial arts training? Or even some gymnastics flips?"

Ivor paused as the idea took shape in his mind. "You're right," he said, excited by the skills they already had. "We can make up our own stuff that nobody else is doing."

So the boys practiced integrating their martial arts and gymnastics skills into their break dancing and "popping" routines. In the process they discovered that they'd created a new, mixed style of dance that was uniquely their own. And, as their dancing skills increased, so did their popularity.

"Go Sean! Go Sean!" a crowd of kids chanted above the music while Sean flipped, spun, and moved his quick feet to the rhythm of the beat. A back flip and a solid landing finished Sean's routine, and the crowd erupted with applause. Sean's opponent conceded his loss with a nod in his direction. Sean wiped the sweat off his forehead and grinned.

"All right, man! That was fresh!" Ivor said loudly into Sean's ear, and then gave him a proud brotherly slap on the shoulder.

Due to a new community program designed by the school to try to keep kids away from gangs and drugs, Sean and Ivor were able to spend their afternoons in the school gym with their friends "battling"—engaging in a freestyle dance competition one-on-one with other kids. The crowd would cheer for each of the performers, and the performer with the loudest cheers won. Sean and Ivor were favorites among their peers and were often the winners of the freestyle "battle."

Friday night parties at Aunt Faye's house were also highly anticipated events, and Sean and Ivor loved the house full of extended relatives and the fun, the lively atmosphere of loud reggae music, and the Jamaican food that continued all night long. Eventually Sean, Ivor, and their cousins would fall asleep in the living room, unable to keep their eyes open any longer, and wake up to breakfast with the adults a few hours later.

"You're here!" Aunt Faye exclaimed over the

throbbing music when they arrived the next Friday night. "Did you bring me a hug?"

The boys hugged Aunt Faye, and then went to find their cousins in the backyard while their parents gathered to visit with the other adults. Dinner sizzled on the hot grill, and the air was heavy with an aroma that made Sean's mouth water. He thrust his hand into the rectangular ice box and retrieved a floating can of cold soda. Some of the neighborhood kids had already set up a dance floor of flattened cardboard, and were dancing. Sean sipped his soda while he watched, but soon the rhythm enticed him, and he put down his drink to dance. Ivor joined him, and together they worked out their complicated routines with natural ease.

Sweat beaded on Sean's forehead as he let his body respond to the music, and before long he and Ivor had an audience that included the amazed adults. They enjoyed the attention and gave a show of their best moves while everyone watched and clapped.

"Did you know our kids could dance like that?" Sean's dad exclaimed in surprise.

Their mom looked just as impressed. "No, I didn't," she answered, her mouth open in amazement. *When* had they become so skilled?

The music ended, everyone applauded, and Sean stood breathless and pleased next to Ivor as his aunts and uncles showered them with compliments.

"Someday you're going to be an entertainer!"

"With skill like that, you're going to be famous!"

Aunt Faye pasted a dollar bill on Sean's sweating forehead and patted him on the cheek. "One of these days I know I'm going to see you dance like that on TV," she said with a wink.

Sean grinned as he peeled the bill off of his forehead and examined it. *Maybe it's a sign,* he thought to himself. *Maybe someday I'll actually be paid to dance.*

The compliments seemed to take on a prophetic air as they implanted in Sean's mind. Aunt Faye's Friday night parties continued to be a practice stage for Sean and Ivor, and as time went on, the thought of being famous someday motivated both of them.

The more immersed Sean became in the hip-hop and reggae world, the more he started to change. Although Sean's mom and dad were proud of the way he had mastered his dance techniques, they were not as pleased with his new look and attitude. Conflicts often arose between him and his parents.

"Sean, your hair is getting too long," Sean's dad complained more than once. "You need to get a haircut." He looked his son up and down with a critical eye. "Maybe I should just take the scissors to you myself. And what is with the baggy pants you wear? You could jump out of an airplane without a parachute and still survive wearing those ridiculous things."

But Sean's world now revolved around the hip-hop and reggae music culture. He wasn't about to change just because his parents weren't "down" with his new style. He looked and acted the part. It was his life now. And he would rather die than give it up.

CHAPTER 5

ean could tell by the look on his father's face that something serious was about to happen, and the feeling in the pit of his stomach warned him that it probably wasn't good news. He glanced at Ivor who sat next to him at the table, and they both looked at their parents with apprehension.

"Your father has an announcement to make," Mom said in a quiet voice.

"I want you to know that I've spent a lot of time thinking about this," Dad began. "And I've decided that it's in our family's best interest to move away from New York."

"What?" Sean felt like someone had knocked the breath out of him. He turned to look at Ivor, whose face was as still as a statue, then back at his parents.

"We're moving to Virginia." Sean's dad finished the announcement with an air of finality.

"Virginia?" Sean repeated in disbelief. "What's in Virginia?"

"Real estate," Sean's dad said. "There is an opportunity to invest in an area that is expected to experience a lot of growth during the next few years, and we are in a position to get in on the ground floor."

"What about our friends? What about Aunt Faye? And the rest of our family? We're just going to pick up and move far away from everyone?" Sean searched his dad's face for evidence of room to negotiate, but found none. His dad's jaw was firmly set, and that usually meant that the subject was not open for discussion. Sean saw tears fill his mother's eyes when he mentioned Aunt Faye, and realized that she wasn't very happy about the idea of moving, either.

"No!" Sean clenched his fist as burning tears came to his eyes. "I'm not moving. I don't want to move. Who cares about the stupid investment opportunity? We're doing fine here."

"That's not the only reason we're moving." Dad sighed, and the crease in his forehead deepened. "I've seen the influence the city has had on you boys. This fast-paced lifestyle isn't healthy. In Jamaica where I grew up, we had fresh, open countryside. It was good. I want you to experience that kind of life."

Sean's dad camped resolutely on the decision he had made, despite Sean and Ivor's best efforts to change his mind. Their belongings were wrapped in newspaper and packed in boxes, pictures came down off the walls, and the furniture was loaded onto a big moving truck. When the job was done, the house was empty of everything except memories. Sadly, Sean and Ivor said goodbye to their South Freeport home for the last time.

Sean stared sullenly out the car window on the way to Virginia, watching the trees and bushes flash by in a blur of green as each highway milepost marker took him farther and farther away from the life he loved. At the age of 15, he wasn't looking forward to starting over in a new town and a new school, and he certainly wasn't interested in making any new friends.

Fredericksburg, Virginia, turned out to be every bit as boring as Sean and Ivor had imagined. Compared to the bright lights, excitement, and energy of the big city in New York, life in Fredericksburg was mundane. They settled into a new house surrounded by trees with no streetlights and no close neighbors.

At school, Sean and Ivor were two of the few Black students, and the only New Yorkers. They wore their New York air with pride, and while their ability to dance made them a lot of friends, it also made them some enemies. The local hip-hop crowd didn't appreciate the newcomers, and a rivalry began to form. Animosity continued to grow like molten lava in a restless volcano, and Sean and Ivor knew that it was a matter of time before a serious confrontation erupted.

"Sean, guess what, man?" Ivor said, brimming with news. He pointed to a guy standing next to him. "We're not the only ones from New York here anymore. Meet Sean Pollard."

"Hey," Sean said with a nod, curious about his brother's new acquaintance.

Sean Pollard, also known as "Vex," was from Brooklyn, New York, and had the gift of rhyme. Instantly, Sean and Ivor liked him, and the three became best friends. With Vex's rap skills and Sean and Ivor's dance skills, they made a great team, and began to perform together at local events. This gave the three New York natives even more popularity; it also made them the recipients of more jealousy from local high school rivals.

One night at a local club, tensions with the local hip-hop crowd reached an all-time high. Ivor had already gone inside the club, and Sean was about to follow when his plans were interrupted by a woman's high-pitched words.

"Sean! Don't even think about hitting my cousin again!"

Sean stopped, for he recognized the taunting voice behind him. The club's noise seemed to fade into nothing as he tuned his every sense to the possibility of movement behind him. Slowly, he turned to face his challenger. It was a girl named Hope with a reputation for causing trouble.

"Hope, what are you doing? I don't even know your cousin," Sean protested.

Hope strode toward him. "Why are you trying to act like you don't know what I'm talking about?" she demanded, slapping his face. Sean clenched his jaw, resisting the urge to retaliate. Her words were having an effect on the crowd of guys near her, and Sean knew he was in for a fight. The group of stone-faced opponents began to shift into position around him, including rivals looking for any excuse to try to take him down. With Ivor in the club already, Sean stood alone and uneasy, muscles tensed for defense.

"Why are you messing with her cousin?" one of the guys demanded.

"I told you, I don't know her cousin. I'm not looking for trouble. I'm just here to dance." Sean started to back away, but he didn't get far.

Sean's adversary made the first move, and then pandemonium broke loose as Sean dodged and struck, trying to defend himself against the band of more than 30 attackers. Moments later he saw Ivor enter the fray with a flying kick in his defense. Party-goers poured out of the club to gather around the fight. The conflict seemed to intensify as the number of assailants increased, and Sean and Ivor quickly worked to fight their way out. Finally they broke free long enough to escape into the now-empty club and bolt the door.

Out of breath and full of adrenalin, Sean and Ivor watched the door bolt shudder as the frenzied mob outside tried to break the door down.

"They're going to break in," Ivor warned.

"You're right," Sean concurred, noting that the hinges were beginning to buckle. "Get ready."

As the two braced for more action they heard the shrill scream of sirens. Just in time, the police arrived to break up the mob. Seeing the reflection of flashing red and blue lights on the windows, Sean breathed a sigh of relief. He knew, however, that this encounter was not going to be the last.

A couple of days later, one of Sean's friends met him in the hallway at school. "So I heard that you and your brother beat up an entire mob on Friday night," he reported with a big grin.

"What?" Sean asked, bending one eyebrow up and laughing.

"The rumor is that you were out clubbing, and a whole group attacked you, and you guys totally wiped them out," his friend continued.

Sean couldn't wait to tell Ivor. They laughed about the ludicrous report together, and decided maybe it wasn't such a bad idea to let the rumor continue to circulate.

"Maybe some of those other guys who want to pick fights with us will think twice after hearing this," Ivor said hopefully.

But Ivor's optimism was misplaced. Instead their winning that fight being a deterrent to other rivals, the new rumor seemed to issue a challenge. They didn't know it, of course, but one of Sean and Ivor's biggest confrontations was still ahead.

CHAPTER 6

Hey, are you one of those dancers from New York?"

Sean pushed his tray down the cafeteria line a few more inches and turned his head to see a pretty girl looking up at him.

"I'm Sean," he nodded, holding out his hand to her.

The girl shook his hand and smiled. "Sue. I saw you perform at the competition the other night. You guys are good. I'm actually from New York, too. Brooklyn," she added, giving the cafeteria cashier her lunch money. "We just moved here." She sighed. "I don't know how I'm going to survive in Virginia."

Sean laughed. "Yeah, I know what you mean, but you'll get used to it. It's not as bad as I first thought. When I got here, I thought I'd never make it. But it's OK here. There are even a couple of good clubs nearby."

"Really." Sue looked surprised. "Where do you usually go clubbing?"

"Richmond," Sean said, sliding into a seat at an empty table. Sue took the seat across from him.

"I'd love to go check them out," she said between bites. "My sisters and I love to dance. We were pretty hard core on the hip-hop scene in Brooklyn."

Vex and Ivor placed their trays on the same table and each grabbed a chair. Sean welcomed them with a smile and introduced them to Sue.

"Why don't you go clubbing with us on Saturday night?" Sean suggested when lunch was over. "Bring your sisters. We'll all go. It'll be fun."

"We'll be there," Sue promised with a wave as she left the cafeteria.

Saturday night clubbing was even more fun with the three girls along. They were just as hard core into hip-hop as they had promised, and the six of them dominated the dance floor all night. Sean was impressed, especially with Sue, and he made sure that most of his evening was spent with her. She seemed to enjoy his company as well. When the lights came on to signal closing time, the new friends stood outside together, reluctant for the night to end.

"We have to do this again," Ivor vowed.

"Definitely. But for tonight, we've got to get home. Come on, girls." Sue yawned into the palm of one of her hands, and motioned to her sisters with the other. "We've got to get up and go to church in the morning."

"Wait, you guys go to church?" Sean asked Sue as the rest of the group meandered toward the cars.

Sue nodded and shrugged. "Yeah. My parents are more into the church thing than I am, but I go with them, and it's cool. I like it."

A familiar feeling of curiosity tickled Sean's mind. "So you must know something about the Bible."

Sue smiled and nodded again. "Well, yeah. Of course."

"Do you think maybe sometime we could—" Sean began.

"Do you want to study the Bible with me, Sean? Is that what you're trying to ask?" Sue laughed. "Yeah, sure. Let's meet at the library on Monday—whoever wants to study together. I'll bring my Bible."

"Looking forward to it," Sean said, smiling down at Sue. He paused. "I had a great time with you tonight."

Sue seemed suddenly shy. "Me too." They smiled at each other for a moment, and then Sue broke the silence. "I'll see you Monday," she said softly, and then she turned to go.

Sean was excited to see Sue on Monday, but he was also intrigued by the opportunity to finally look through the pages of the book he knew so little about, with someone willing to help him understand it. Ivor and Vex were interested as well, so the four of them got together, this time in the library to study the Bible.

Sean listened eagerly while Sue opened up her Bible and started to talk.

"Really, this whole story starts in heaven," Sue said. "There was this really beautiful angel named Lucifer. He was one of God's special angels, but then he got jealous of God and wanted all the angels to worship him instead of God. So he started talking behind God's back, trying to make God look bad and himself look good. About a third of the angels believed him and turned against God."

"What did God do?" Sean asked.

Sue turned in her Bible to Revelation 12. "Well," she continued, "there was war in heaven, and Lucifer and his angels lost, and were forced out of heaven. He came to this earth, and he's now known as Satan, or the devil."

"Why didn't God just destroy him?" Ivor asked.

"Probably because God is totally committed to letting people have freedom of choice," Sue guessed. "Plus, if God had killed Satan, then probably the other angels still in heaven would have served Him out of fear instead of out of love, and I don't think God wanted that."

Sean leaned forward. "What happened after he came to this earth?"

Sue leafed back through her Bible until she found Genesis. "Well, God had created the first humans, Adam and Eve, and they were living here in a beautiful garden. God confined Satan to one tree, and warned Adam and Eve to stay away from it. If they ate the fruit of the tree, they would die."

"Let me guess," Vex said. "They didn't listen."

"You guessed it." Sue sighed. "Satan was able to fool them into thinking that God wasn't who He said He was, just like he had with some of the angels. It was really sad, because the earth and the people were cursed by sin, and everything started to die."

Sean folded his arms and leaned back in his chair. "What did God do?"

"He's pretty much been defending His reputation ever since," Sue continued. "He came up with a plan that would defend His honor and break the curse once and for all so He could eventually make everything new. He sent His Son to take the curse of the whole world on Himself and pay for it all by dying on a cross. It's here, in John 3:16: 'For God so loved the world that he gave his one and only Son, that whoever believes in him shall not perish, but have eternal life'" (NIV).

"Jesus," Sean said quietly.

"Jesus," Sue repeated with a nod. "But God is still into the whole idea of freedom of choice, so He still doesn't force people. It's up to each person individually whether they believe in Him or not."

"One more question." Vex looked at Sue intently. "What's the deal with the devil? What is he doing now?"

"He's doing his best to distract us from God," Sue paused, "and destroy us. My dad says that we won't realize how many times God has protected us from Satan's attempts to kill us until we get to heaven and our angels tell us about it."

The puzzle pieces were starting to come together in Sean's mind as he pondered what Sue had said. He thought about his family's close call with the drug lords in Jamaica when he was a little kid, and realized that Satan had stirred up that dangerous situation. Even though they didn't know about God at the time, God had protected their lives. It was a sobering thought.

Through the end of school and all summer long, Sean and Sue and the others continued to meet on the weekends to go to the clubs, and at other times to study more of the Bible. The more Sean learned, the more interested in spirituality he became, and he began to explore the beliefs of different religions, as well as his Jamaican cultural roots.

★ ★ ★

One afternoon while in town with his family, Sean discovered a surf shop. As he browsed through the sandals, hats, and surfing equipment he noticed a green, yellow, and black Jamaican belt.

The colors of the Jamaican flag, Sean thought. *Cool.*

Sean purchased the belt, and met his family at the car. As they drove along, Sean took the belt out to look at it again.

Just then his dad looked at him in the rearview mirror. "Sean, is that a Jamaican belt you have there?"

"Yeah," Sean nodded. "I just bought it."

"Give it to me."

Sean handed the belt to his father, who immediately tossed it out the window! Sean stared at him, stunned.

"Ronnie, what did you do that for?" Mom exclaimed.

"I know where this is all going," Dad said firmly as he rolled up his window. "First it's the Jamaican belt, then comes the Bob Marley T-shirt, then the dreadlocks. Next thing you know, he'll be smoking the ganja."

"Ganja—marijuana? Are you kidding? Dad, you don't know what you're talking about," Sean insisted, angry about the loss of his belt. He decided in his mind that as soon as he got the chance, he was going to buy another belt just like it. *Maybe two,* he thought rebelliously. And as time passed Sean continued to buy things that to him were innocent, but that reminded his father of the Jamaican drug culture. And every time his dad saw that Sean had something like that he confiscated it and threw it away. But this only fueled Sean's determination, and he always found a way to buy more.

Summer was soon over, and Sean's senior year began. Ivor now attended college at Virginia State University, and it felt strange to Sean to not have his brother with him at school every day. He still got together with Ivor and Vex on the weekends, and they continued to practice their dance routines together. Their winning performances still swept local talent shows, and even though they were tired of fighting, their proud refusal to back down from a challenge often landed them in fist-to-fist conflicts with rivaling groups. And Sean and Sue began spending more time together, sometimes just hanging out, sometimes studying the Bible.

One night, with Ivor at college, Sean was home alone. His parents had gone away for the weekend. Bored, and tired of being by himself, Sean decided to call Sue and invite her to come over. They'd just settled onto the couch with a bag of potato chips and a movie video when they heard a loud banging at the door.

Startled, Sean jumped up off the couch and standing at the edge of the window carefully peeked around to see who was there. Sue crept to the other side. They saw two of Sean's rivals pounding on the door and calling his name. Sean recognized one of them, a guy named Shorty who had threatened him before.

"Sean! We know you're in there! Get out here!"

Sean could hear raucous laughter as the guys
yelled threats to him and demanded that he come out.
Each time they slammed against the screen door, Sean
became more incensed. Sue backed away from the
window, biting her lower lip as she looked helplessly
at Sean.

"Who's in there with you, Sean? Come on out
here and face us!"

Sean's heart raced, and he clenched his hands into
fists. "Who do they think they are?" he said out loud.
Sean knew he could take them both in a fight, but not
if they were armed. With that in mind, he turned and
ran up the stairs to his father's gun closet. Pulling out
a black pistol, he snapped the clip into place and dis-
engaged the safety as he walked down the steps to the
living room.

Sue's eyes widened at the sight of the gun. "Sean!
What are you going to do?"

Sean didn't answer as he walked calmly toward
the door.

"Sean! Don't!" Sue pleaded with frightened tears in
her voice. She put her hand on the gun and looked up
at Sean. "Please, Sean. Don't do this. Just trust God."

"Trust God?"

Sean stopped abruptly and looked at Sue, then
down at the gun he was carrying. He wasn't sure
why, but he lowered the gun and sat down to think.
Sue sat next to him, crying softly.

A few minutes later, the banging on the door
ceased, and Sean could hear retreating footsteps as
the guys outside walked off the porch. After several

minutes, Sean peeked out the window. The yard was empty.

"It looks like they're gone." Sean let the curtains fall back into place. "They could be hiding in the bushes, though."

He reached for the phone to call Ivor. "Man, you're not going to believe what just happened here," he said, recounting the story to Ivor while Sue listened.

"What?" Ivor's voice was angry. "It's time for those little punks to learn a lesson."

At that, Sue grabbed her sweater. "Sean, I need to go home," she said, standing up and turning toward the door.

"No!" Sean insisted. "What if they're still out there?"

"They're gone, Sean. And besides, if I don't get home soon, my parents are going to be upset."

Reluctantly, Sean hung up the phone and walked Sue to her car before retreating back inside the house. His ears were tuned to every noise as he turned down the lights and sat alone, wondering if the intruders would be back for another round. The second hand ticked circles around the clock as time passed.

He'd fallen asleep, for Sean woke up suddenly to the sound of cars in the driveway. The door burst open, and Ivor and five carloads of friends came running into the house.

"Have they been back?" Ivor questioned. Sean shook his head, still in a daze, and Ivor led his friends up the stairs. A moment later, they came back down armed with loaded weapons from the gun closet.

Everything seemed to be in slow motion as Sean watched from the couch.

"Come on, get in the car." Ivor motioned for Sean to follow. "We're going to end this once and for all. Let's get them!"

They had never gotten into a fight with guns before. Sean tried not to think about Sue's pleading words, or about the consequences that could follow their actions.

What if something happens tonight? His heart pounded out the words. *If the cops don't catch you, your parents will. Either way, you're dead.*

Sean paused, the weight of the decision heavy on his chest. Then, with a deep breath, he grabbed the loaded pistol and ran out the door.

CHAPTER 7

Quietly, Ivor motioned Sean and each of his friends into position behind bushes as they surrounded Shorty's house with guns cocked.

"Wait here," Ivor commanded in a whisper. "Two of us will go up to the door. When he comes out, we do our thing."

Sean held his breath in the shadow of the bushes and clamped a sweaty palm around the cold grip of the gun as Ivor and a friend scrambled silently up the steps. Sean looked down at the trigger, his stomach fluttering at the thought of unleashing the explosive power that lay dormant inside the chamber.

"Shorty!" Ivor shouted, as he banged rapidly on the door. "Open up! I want to talk to you! Whatever you had in mind to say to my little brother earlier you can come out here and say to me now. "

Sean searched the dark windows for a sign of movement, but saw none. After a few minutes of pounding on the door, Ivor and his friend came down off the porch.

"I don't think anybody's home." Ivor seemed dejected with the result of their incomplete mission.

"Ivor, let's get out of here," Sean said in a low voice. "Somebody's going to see us and word is going to spread. We might already be in too deep."

The friends piled back into the cars and squealed away into the night. Sean rode along in the backseat feeling strangely relieved that no one had been home. Even so, he was still worried that someone had seen them and would tell Shorty they had been at his house. If Shorty knew they'd been there things could get only worse.

Although there were no immediate repercussions for their actions, Sean knew it was best to lay low. He didn't attend any parties or go to any clubs. He was certain that if the story made the rounds, Shorty might decide to strike first. And Sean wasn't ready to die.

Things seemed to quiet down the next year when Sean began attending a college near Ivor. Sue and her sisters had moved away, and Sean, Vex, and Ivor focused their attention on their music and dancing. Sean enjoyed the new challenges college life had to offer as well as the freedom from his parents.

One night, while on the phone, Ivor surprised Sean with a question. "Do you ever wonder what would happen to you if you died?"

Sean silently cradled the phone against his ear for a moment before answering. "Yeah," he admitted. "I mean, some people, when they die, they seem like they have this peace about the whole thing. Like it's OK because they know where they're headed. I don't have that. Do you?"

"Nope." Ivor's voice sounded distant. "I've been thinking about it, though, ever since that night we went to Shorty's house."

"Me too." Sean stared at the ceiling.

Sean could hear Ivor yawn on the other end of the phone. "Well, I guess I'd better go," Ivor said sleepily. "Talk to you later."

After the phone call ended, Sean lay in his bed, trying to wrap his mind around the subject of life and death. He knew that the answer must be buried somewhere in everything he'd studied in the Bible. He just hadn't found it yet. At least, not the answer he was looking for.

It was during that school year that Sean, Ivor, and Vex met someone new. Mondo McCann was new to Virginia State University, and with rhyming ability that complemented Vex's skill, he was quickly assimilated into the group, and the four became fast friends. Vex and Mondo wrote lyrics and rapped, and Sean and Ivor danced to the rhythm.

"We should come up with a name," Mondo suggested one day while they practiced a new song. "What should we call ourselves?"

The four thought for a moment, and then Ivor tossed an idea out for the group to consider. "Back in high school they used to call us Vex 1 and the Boogiemonsters. How about if the four of us just call ourselves the Boogiemonsters?"

"It still fits," Vex said, nodding. "Boogie works because we know how to get down and party."

"Yeah, and Monsters works because of our tough 'don't mess with us' kind of image," Sean added with a laugh.

Mondo smiled. "Looks like we've got ourselves a name."

The new name seemed to unify them in purpose, and they set their sights on success. Their music and dance showed new intensity on stage, and they won first place in every competition they entered. Sean often thought about the years before when he'd preformed at Aunt Faye's house in Queens, and he silently promised himself that someday her prediction of seeing him dance on TV would come true. For now, things were looking good.

One night Sean was getting ready to go to bed when his phone rang. It was Ivor.

"Hey, Susan is in New York City on business for a few days. She wants us to come visit her," Ivor announced.

"Susan," Sean said. "She's back here from England? Great! When does she want to see us?"

"Well, that's the weird thing." Ivor hesitated. "She . . . well, she wants us to come right now."

"But it's like 9:00 o'clock at night right now, and it's a six-hour drive," Sean argued. "Isn't that kind of late to be driving from Virginia to New York?"

"Yeah, I know. That's what I said, too. But she says it's important, and her voice sounded weird, so I agreed to go. Are you game?"

Sean agreed, and soon found himself in the passenger seat of Ivor's car. *This is crazy*, he thought as they merged onto the empty freeway. Equally-spaced yellow lights suspended over the road illuminated spheres on the pavement and reflected off the windshield in hypnotic rhythm. Sean found himself becoming sleepier with each passing mile. Unable to keep his eyes open any longer, he soon fell asleep.

He awoke to Ivor shaking him. "We're here, man. Wake up."

Sean groggily opened his eyes and stretched his legs as far as the floorboard would let him. They had been driving all night, and now it was early morning. "Might as well go in," Ivor said. Susan welcomed them with smiles and hugs, as they went into the house and sank down on the couch. She sat down across from them and gave them a long, serious look before speaking.

"The Lord wants both of you to give your lives to him and be baptized." she said, and the words were more a plea than a statement. "If you guys were to die, what would happen to you?"

Sean was surprised to hear the question that had been on his mind repeated out loud by his cousin. A strange sense of urgency came over him, and he looked at Ivor, wondering if his brother felt it, too.

Both young men were silent on the way home to Virginia. It was strange how Susan had urgently insisted that they come immediately to see her. Her request that they give their lives to the Lord was even stranger. Sean had known about Susan's interest in God and the Bible since they were kids, but she had never been pushy before. His thoughts tumbled through his mind like popcorn on high heat.

Ivor started to speak, then paused and shifted uncomfortably in his seat as he gripped the steering wheel with both hands. "Sean, I have something to say that might sound strange."

"Well, you wouldn't be the only one saying strange things lately." Sean half chuckled as he thought of Susan's request. "So go ahead."

Ivor glanced toward Sean. "I don't think the devil wanted us to hear what Susan had to say to us."

"What?" Sean shook his head, confused. "Why would you think that?"

"Because both of us were almost killed last night."

"Almost killed? What do you mean?"

"I mean," Ivor continued, "that while I was driving last night this heavy grogginess came over me and I couldn't resist it. When I woke up the car was going over some bumps, and it took me a second to realize that I was still driving. I looked down at the speedometer and we were going 70 miles per hour, but we weren't on the road anymore."

Sean felt his mouth go dry as he listened to the story. He swallowed and watched Ivor's face.

"Branches started hitting the windshield," Ivor remembered, shaking his head. "I realized that the freeway was to the left of us, and I was able to get control of the steering wheel and maneuver us back onto the road. But Sean, what I'm trying to tell you is that if the wheel had turned to the right even slightly, we would have hit a tree at 70 miles per hour. There's no way we would have survived. I think the devil tried to kill us."

Sean felt goose bumps on his arms. He had no idea that his life was almost cut short. Wildly, he thought that he could have been killed in his sleep and never even known it. A deep sense of awareness flooded Sean, and he realized that they weren't just fighting against neighborhood kids or hip-hop rivals.

This battle was on another whole playing field with a force they couldn't see. A force that for some reason wanted them dead.

"The thing is," Ivor added thoughtfully, "we weren't killed. We weren't even hurt. God must have protected us from it."

Sean shook his head, amazed. God had saved their lives—but for what reason? Something big was happening. He could feel it.

CHAPTER 8

Remember that guy on campus I told you about who is a huge religious freak; the one who always walks around wearing headphones and talking about Bible prophecy?" Ivor asked Sean one afternoon. They were taking a short break from rehearsing dance moves for their next big competition.

Sean took a sip of orange juice and nodded. "Yeah. What about him?"

"I actually had a pretty serious talk with him."

Sean laughed. "In public?"

"Not exactly," Ivor admitted. "It was in the middle of the night. I'm pretty sure that nobody saw."

"Oh, good," Sean put his hand over his heart in mock relief. "Your reputation as campus tough guy is safe."

Ivor didn't laugh. "This is important, Sean. Yesterday I saw something that really shook me up, and I needed someone to talk to."

Sean flipped a metal chair around and straddled it, leaning forward on his elbows. "What did you see?"

"I went for a walk over to some apartments near campus where one of my friends lives," Ivor began. "I'd just turned the corner to go into the parking lot, and there was this woman lying in the street. Just lying there, not moving or anything."

"Was she drunk or something?" Sean wondered aloud, trying to picture the scene in his head.

"That's what I thought, too," Ivor continued. "So I just walked around her and headed on toward my friend's house. When I left there I came back around the corner, and she was still lying there. But by this time an ambulance had arrived, and they had covered her body with a sheet. Turns out, she was dead. She'd been stabbed. It was something drug-related, I found out later."

"No wonder you were freaked out. That would have freaked me out too," Sean said, shuddering at the gruesome thought.

"The first thing that came into my mind was, *That woman was unprepared to die.* I just started thinking about everything, you know? I was lying there in my bed and I couldn't sleep." Ivor shrugged. "I knew that *I* was not prepared to die. All I could think about was that weird guy with headphones. And I just had to talk to him."

"So what did you do? Just show up and knock on his door in the middle of the night?" Sean said, half joking.

"That's actually pretty much how it happened," Ivor nodded. "He opened the door and looked at me, and I just stood there and said, 'Look man, you know something. Tell me what it is. What do I need to do to be saved?' And he stepped back and let me in."

"Did he tell you anything?" Sean asked, his interest mounting.

"Yeah. He showed me some texts in the Bible about believing on Jesus, and then asked me if I wanted to let Jesus in my heart. Then he told me to repeat after him while he prayed, and that was it."

"That was it?" Sean asked incredulously. "It was that easy? You're saved now?"

Ivor nodded. "As far as I know. I still think we need to be baptized, though, you and me," he said. "We've got to find a church that will baptize us."

Sean thought it sounded like a good idea, so the two of them found a phone book and began calling the numbers of local churches.

"Here's one." Sean pointed to the listing, and Ivor dialed the number.

"Hello, I'm interested in being baptized," Ivor said into the phone. "Have to take Bible studies first? Oh. Well, no thank you then."

"Find another one," Ivor directed, shaking his head as he hung up the phone.

Sean pointed to another listing. "Try this one."

Ivor dialed, and then listened. "Hello, I'm interested in being baptized." He paused. "I see. I'd have to attend your baptism class first? Uh-huh. I see. OK then. Thanks anyway."

Sean and Ivor went down the list in the phone book, calling number after number, but each church wanted them to study the Bible or take special classes before they would allow them to be baptized.

"This is ridiculous," Ivor complained, increasingly irritable after several phone calls. "I just want to get baptized!"

Sean offered him another number, and he dialed.

"Hello, my brother and I are interested in being baptized, but we don't want to have to take a bunch

Bible studies or attend any special classes first," Ivor
said emphatically. He paused, then brightened. "We
can? Without taking Bible studies or anything first?
Great! We'll be there." Ivor gave Sean a thumbs-up
sign and turned back to the phone. "OK then, we'll
see you on Sunday!"

The next Sunday morning Sean and Ivor stood at
the front of a local church and professed their faith in
Jesus in front of the congregation. Then the pastor
baptized them in the little baptismal tank. A sermon
followed. The choir sang to close the service, and
they went home.

"I don't feel any different," Sean admitted that
evening. "I don't feel changed or renewed or re-
born—or anything like that pastor talked about."

"I don't know how I'm supposed to feel. All I
know is I feel relieved," his brother told him. "Now
if something happens to me while I'm at a party or in
a fight, and I die, I know I'm covered."

Sean shrugged and nodded, but on the inside, he
felt sure that something was still missing. He didn't
have much time to think about it, though. For the
next few months the four members of the
Boogiemonsters spent every waking moment practicing for the Howard University competition in
Washington, D.C. This was their next big step, and
they all knew it. It was time to face the big time.

CHAPTER 9

Winter hit the East Coast with arctic fury, and the Boogiemonsters felt every icy blast of wind that whistled and slammed around the Volkswagen windows. It was a two-hour trip to Washington, D.C. for the Howard University talent show, and to the Boogiemonsters it seemed like they were trapped in a freezer the entire way.

"I'm going to freeze to death," Sean complained, tapping on the temperature control under the dashboard. "Can't this thing pump out any heat?"

"No!" Ivor grouched. He sat hunched over the steering wheel, fingers locked in a frozen, white-knuckled grip. He blew a hot circle into the steam that fogged up the windshield and continued to drive the icy roads in silence.

"Any idea where we're going to sleep when we get there?" Vex asked, teeth chattering. Wearing jackets, hats, and gloves, he and Mondo shivered in the backseat.

"I'm afraid we're going to have to snuggle up in the car tonight." Ivor shared the bad news through blue lips as his three passengers groaned. "We don't have anywhere else to stay. Sorry guys."

After a near-sleepless night in the below-freezing Volkswagen, the Boogiemonsters were dismayed to discover that they were scheduled to be the first performers in the talent show.

"This is not good," Ivor said, shaking his head. "Thirty different groups are competing. They'll have forgotten all about us by the end of the competition."

"We'll just have to make sure they can't forget about us," Mondo said with determination, and the others nodded agreement. They hadn't spent countless hours practicing, driven two hours on a treacherous highway, and spent a sleepless night in near-zero temperatures just to bomb in the most important competition they'd ever done.

The Boogiemonsters were ready! When their name was called the four college students ran out, the music started—and they owned the stage. They gave the crowd and the judges the best performance they could muster. Then it was over. They found seats in the audience so they could size up their competition. There were 29 more acts to go.

Sean's heart sank when he saw the professional skill of the other groups. It was easy for them to sweep the smaller competitions, but here at Howard University many of these groups were at the top of their game. They'd known the competition would be tough, but they hadn't realized how tough. The Boogiemonsters were up against serious competitors.

"Do you think we have a chance?" Sean whispered to Ivor.

"Of course we do," Ivor said into Sean's ear. "We haven't practiced our whole lives for nothing. We're just as good as anybody else. We've got a shot at this."

Sean hoped Ivor was right, but he couldn't help feeling nervous as the last group finished and the winners were announced. He held his breath.

"The third runner up—" A group's name was called. Sean leaned forward, looking at each of the Boogiemonsters, not sure if they should be worried or relieved that they didn't receive third place.

"The second runner up—" Another group took the stage to the sound of applause, and then came the moment of truth.

"The first place winners are—"

The announcer paused. It seemed that the whole auditorium held its breath.

"First place goes to—The Boogiemonsters!"

At that, Sean wanted to jump up and down with joy. Instead, he followed the other guys as they walked confidently and coolly onto the stage to receive their recognition. The crowd went wild as the four stood before them.

Afterward, the Boogiemonsters were inundated with attention. Reporters crowded around them to ask questions and to get the scoop on this hot new group from Virginia that had just taken the Howard University talent show by storm.

In the midst of the sweet delirium of the spotlight, the Boogiemonsters were greeted by a man wearing a suit. "Gentlemen, I was impressed by your performance tonight," he said as he shook each of their hands. "I personally believe that you could be the next big act in the music industry, and with your permission, I'd like to arrange financing for a four-song demo album. I'm willing to bet my own money that if your unique style of music is shopped among the major recording labels in New York, you'll find yourselves with a recording contract. I'll give you my card. We'll be in touch."

The man walked away, and the Boogiemonsters looked at each other, intoxicated with the taste of fame, and the tangible possibility of making it big.

Ivor looked as though he'd like to burst into dance right there. "We're so close to what we've always wanted. I can feel it in my bones. Money, fame, attention, big house, a car with a heater—did I mention money?"

"This is huge!" Mondo gasped as he examined the man's business card. "I still can't believe it—we're going to do a demo. It's like a dream."

The dream soon became a reality for all of them. While driving back and forth to the studio in Hampton, Virginia, and spending long hours recording didn't turn out to be as glamorous as they'd expected, the possibility of success kept them motivated.

"I hope we're not wasting our time," Sean moaned one night after a long recording session. "You know that everybody in New York is trying to get signed. There's no way they're going to listen to us. Can you even guess how many of these demos get processed in one day?"

But Mondo told the guys that he knew someone who knew someone in New York City who was going to get him an appointment with a management agency. While the other guys continued their college studies, Mondo traveled to New York shopping the demo wherever he could. Several months passed.

Finally, one day, Mondo had an announcement. "Rush Studios is interested in us. They want us all to come up. This is it!" he promised.

Sean and the others traveled to New York to meet with a potential manager named Derrick and his partner Francesca at Rush Studios—the same place where artists like Run DMC and LL Cool J had gotten their start in the music business.

Derrick and Fran listened to the demo songs the Boogiemonsters had produced, and said they were confident they could help get them a deal. And so the Boogiemonsters signed a contract, and then left New York to go home and wait.

CHAPTER 10

Six days after signing with Rush Studios, the telephone rang. By the time the call ended the Boogiemonsters had an appointment to interview with the President of Pendulum/EMI Records.

It felt strange to be standing in the plush interior of a high-rise New York office building overlooking 6th Avenue. Sean thought about all of the famous artists who had probably stood in this exact place for the same reason, and wondered if this would be the beginning for the Boogiemonsters as well.

The president of the record company entered the room, greeted them, then sat back in his chair and began to ask questions. He seemed impressed with their answers. "OK, now," he said. "Let me see your visual performance."

The Boogiemonsters poured their hearts into the music and motion, giving their audience of one the show of a lifetime. When it was over, they waited in breathless anticipation as he pondered the group that stood before him. The slow seconds stretched into minutes. At last he spoke.

"I think you have something. I'd like to welcome you to the Pendulum/EMI Records family by offering you an eight-record deal," he told them. "I'm assuming you're interested—why else would you be here? So let's move on to discuss the contract."

The Boogiemonsters listened with barely contained enthusiasm as the details of their contract were laid out before them. They would receive $150,000 to make the first album, and more money with each successive recording. In addition, money would be coming in from performances and record sales. The numbers were staggering to Sean as he listened in disbelief to what was being offered. "We'll release a single and a video of one of your songs to whet the audience's appetite while we work on your first album," the president decided. "By the time your album is released, everybody will know about the Boogiemonsters." He looked at them with a smile. "I hope you're ready, because the whirlwind is about to begin."

When they were alone again, the guys jumped up and down, mouths open in silent screams. Everything they had ever wanted culminated in this moment. They were being offered more money than they had ever seen in their lives to do something they loved. The door to fame had finally opened. There was only one thing that could possibly hold them back from their dreams: Mom and Dad.

Dad shook his head firmly. "No way."

"What about college? What about your future?" Mom argued. "You can't throw it all away for what could turn out to be nothing."

"It's not for nothing, Mom," Ivor promised. "We've really got a chance at this. Just give us some time to prove it."

Dad and Mom were unrelenting until they received a call from the president of Pendulum/EMI Records himself. Sean and Ivor watched anxiously to see if the phone call would change their fate. When he hung up the phone, Dad sighed as he looked at Mom, then back at Sean and Ivor. "One semester," he conceded. "I'll give you one semester."

"One semester is all we need," Ivor said confidently.

In the big studio on 42nd Avenue for the first time, the Boogiemonsters arrived ready to begin work on their first single. The recording session was at night, and the studio lights were dim as the four walked out of the elevator and into the studio. Sean stared at the rows of buttons and lights on the studio equipment in the recording booth.

"Pretty impressive, huh?"

Sean turned to see a White guy with long hair standing behind him. "I'm Bill—the sound engineer."

Sean smiled and nodded at Bill.

Bill's long hair, blue jeans, and heavy metal T-shirt told Sean that Bill was more of a hard rock fan, and Sean wondered if Bill was the right choice to mix their rap/hip-hop/reggae blend of music. But when Bill went to work with them in the studio, Sean's skepticism vanished immediately. Bill was definitely a professional.

Vex and Mondo took turns rapping into the microphone while Bill listened intently, commenting, praising, and asking them to repeat takes where necessary.

"Hey, how about we layer it like this?" Bill

pushed the playback button, and the sounds of the freshly-recorded Boogiemonsters filled the studio.

The performers looked at each other with wide, happy grins.

Bill smiled at their excitement. "Like what you hear?"

"This guy might be into rock, but he sure knows hip-hop," Sean said to Ivor as they watched Bill pull the takes together for a tight sound.

"These guys know what they're doing." Ivor smiled at Sean. "We're in the industry now, man."

By the time their first single, "Recognize Thresholds of Negative Stress," hit the airways the Boogiemonsters were already set to work on their first video.

"I've got some ideas for your video," Derrick said. As their manager, he was quite involved with their work. "I've got the shoot scheduled, but first we've got to get you dressed for success."

Derrick led Sean, Ivor, Vex, and Mondo to a room the size of a warehouse that was full of clothing. Sean blinked. The huge room was packed with rows and rows of clothes and accessories.

"Wow." Ivor whistled. "We can pick from here?"

"Yep," Derrick answered. "Try on anything you want. You'll need several outfits, so don't be shy. Let's do this."

Soon the Boogiemonsters were having the time of their lives experimenting with different ensembles with wild colors and crazy styles, strolling for the mirrors and each other until they had a huge pile of possibilities for the video shoot.

Even though it was winter in New York, the shoot was held in an open field. But the Boogiemonsters hardly noticed the frigid temperatures. Excitement kept Sean and Ivor warm as they performed martial arts moves and danced for the camera. Every moment spent as kids practicing on flattened cardboard boxes and performing in the gym for their friends had prepared them for this moment. It was their time to shine.

And then their music and video was released. The demand for the Boogiemonsters exploded, and the guys found themselves continually in the spotlight. It was exciting to see their families' reactions, especially that of Aunt Faye, when their music video played on television. She loved it!

But the Boogiemonsters had no time to rest and enjoy the praise and pride. Now that they were riding the wave of popularity, it was time to begin the long process of creating the rest of the album.

"We need a gimmick," Sean said the day they all sat down to brainstorm for their new record.

Vex put down his pen and looked up at Sean. "What do you mean?"

"Well, think about it," he explained. "Every rap artist has a gimmick. Look at Biggie Smalls—he has the whole 1920's mobster theme. Kriss-Kross—they wear their clothes backwards. You know. A gimmick."

"I see what you mean," Mondo nodded. "We need something that will help us stand out. Something that makes our fans remember us."

"I can't believe we got signed without a gimmick, actually," Sean continued.

"We are unique," Ivor said. "I think that's part of why people keep saying our music is refreshing. It's because everybody's doing gangsta rap right now, with lyrics that encourage violence and put women down, and our stuff is positive. Plus, with the combination of rap and reggae and martial arts, we're definitely going to make our mark."

"True." Sean bit his lip as he thought. "Still, I think we need something more."

The guys sat around the room in silence, thinking.

"Wait!" Vex brightened. "Ivor, remember when we were at that guy's house a few years ago listening to some music, and in one of the songs we heard this dark voice repeating Scripture? It had a really intriguing sound. What if we incorporated the gospel into our music, like quotes from Revelation and stuff, and basically made that part of our gimmick?"

Ivor looked at Vex, eyebrows knit. Thinking. "It was edgy," he said slowly. "I liked it."

"Sounds cool," Mondo agreed. "Maybe we should play around with some lyrics and see how it works."

The guys pulled out a Bible and began to dig around for ideas to use in crafting their rhymes. Not shallow, surface lyrics, but deep, meaningful lyrics that would inspire and teach.

After all his caution, Sean and Ivor's dad was excited about their success, but his fatherly pride urged them to do more. "Are you guys going to dance for the rest of your life?" he asked one day. "Or are you ever going to rap?"

"We're the dancers, Dad. That's what we do," Sean responded. "Besides, the thought of having a microphone in front of my face makes me panic. I'm satisfied just to dance."

Sean thought Ivor felt the same way, but it turned out that he was wrong. "We need to go on the microphone, too," Ivor told him.

"What? No way! Please," Sean said. "We can just dance. We don't need to rap, we don't need to do interviews, we don't have to face people. We can just be the dancers in the back."

"No, man. We've got to go on the mic," Ivor insisted.

"Isn't it a little late to be getting started now?" Sean sighed, knowing from experience that Ivor was going to be able to talk him into it one way or another. "I mean, most rap artists brag about how they've been on the mic for years. We've only played around with it. We are already signed, and we don't really know how to rhyme very well, much less freestyle. We're doomed. If anyone finds out that we've never rapped, nobody's going to listen to us."

"Then I guess we'll have to get real good, real fast." Ivor was not willing to back down. "We need to be sharing what we've learned about the Bible. It's irresponsible for us not to be on the mic."

So Sean and Ivor spent the summer learning to rap. To Sean's surprise, both he and Ivor quickly picked up on the skill. Even though Sean loved rap music, he felt drawn to reggae, and began working to perform a reggae style of rap called chanting. By the end of the summer, Sean and Ivor were performing on stage as rappers with Mondo and Vex as though they had been doing it for years.

CHAPTER 11

The Boogiemonsters adjusted very quickly to life with money. The four guys and a whole group of their friends moved into a house in Laurelton, Queens, and the party lifestyle began. The Boogiemonsters rode the subway into Manhattan every night to record their new album.

Almost in succession, as if it were a train that had started rolling and couldn't stop, the very things their father had predicted years before began to surface in their lives. There were the Bob Marley T-shirts, the dreadlocks, even the marijuana. Sean and Ivor and their friends would kick back, smoking marijuana, and discuss philosophical things. The calm, detached sensation they had while they were high made them feel that their conversations were wise and profound. One of their favorite topics to discuss while stoned was the book of Revelation. Often, they would ponder the same questions about the mark of the beast and 666 that they had wondered about as kids, thinking that perhaps now in their altered state, they would be able to discern more and unlock the secrets in the mysterious book.

"Now this is the way it's supposed to be," Sean said to the guys as they cruised downtown in a limousine. "I don't think I've ever had this many clothes in my entire life."

"No kidding, man," Ivor said. "Look at this." He held up a magazine. "We've got our faces in *Rolling Stone, Vibe, The Source*—everybody wants a piece."

"Revolutionary!" Vex said with a big smile. "That's what they're calling us."

"I saw our video on MTV the other day. It played right after one of Biggie Smalls' songs." Mondo sat back in the soft leather seat and closed his eyes. "Everybody wants to know us. Our house is a non-stop party."

"You've got that right." Ivor shook his head in amazement. "The other day at home I actually stepped over someone sleeping on our floor, partied out. The weird thing is I didn't even know who it was!"

Finished in the studio for the day, the friends headed back to the house to party.

"Hey, guys," one of their friends motioned for them when they came into their place. "I got someone here for you to meet. His name's 'D'. He's cool."

D stuck out his hand, and Sean shook it. "Hey," Sean said with a nod. "Make yourself at home."

Someone lit a joint and began to pass it around. The mood of the room changed as blue smoke filled the air, and everyone seemed to melt into the scenery.

"Let's read Revelation again," Ivor suggested. "Where it talks about last day events."

Sean passed some Bibles around the room, and everyone turned to the back of the book to read.

"So you guys study the Bible a lot?" D asked as he thumbed through the pages.

They nodded.

"I have a question for you then," D continued. "What day do you think the Sabbath is?"

"Sunday." The answer was unanimous around the room.

"Wrong," D said. "Let me ask you another question. What day is the first day of the week?"

Ivor pulled a calendar off the wall and looked at it. "According to this, the first day of the week is Sunday."

"Good," D agreed. "Now listen up. The fourth commandment in the Bible is found in Exodus 20:8. It goes like this: 'Remember the Sabbath day by keeping it holy. Six days you shall labor and do all your work, but the seventh day is a Sabbath to the Lord your God. On it you shall not do any work, neither you, nor your son or daughter, nor your manservant or maidservant, nor your animals, nor the alien within your gates. For in six days the Lord made the heavens and the earth, the sea, and all that is in them, but he rested on the seventh day. Therefore the Lord blessed the Sabbath day and made it holy'" (NIV).

When D finished, the room was silent as the group stared at him with open mouths. "Did you just quote that whole thing from memory?" Sean asked, intrigued.

"Yeah," D nodded. "But did you catch which day God blessed as the Sabbath?"

There was a pause.

"The seventh day," someone said.

"What day of the week is the seventh day?" D asked.

Ivor looked at the calendar he still held in his

hand. "It's Saturday."

Ivor looked at Sean, then back at D. "That's the same conclusion our Uncle Tony came to when he read the Bible," Ivor remembered out loud. Excitement lit his face. "I remember him telling us that when we were just kids."

"It's straight out of the Bible," D said with a shrug. "Your Uncle Tony was right. Saturday is the Sabbath."

Ivor leaned forward. "Don't hold out on us, man. Tell us everything you know."

D began answering questions by quoting more Scripture from memory. Everyone was amazed at his knowledge and understanding of the Bible, and Sean was thrilled to find that the Bible often answers its own questions. Excited, Sean and Ivor and the others often invited D to come over and talk about Scripture with them. As usual, they smoked marijuana as they studied.

★ ★ ★

"Are you guys ready for your performance tonight?" Derrick asked as the Boogiemonsters climbed into the limousine.

"I've been ready since before I could tie my shoes," Vex laughed. "Let's do this."

The club was packed, and the Boogiemonsters stood in the back scanning the crowd.

"Is that who I think it is?" Mondo leaned in and whispered to Sean as he discretely pointed with his thumb.

Sean squinted and looked in the direction Mondo

pointed. "It's the Fugees! Man, that's Lauryn Hill!" Sean thought his chest would explode from excitement when he realized that some of his favorite music artists were in the crowd to watch them perform.

The crowd was alive as the Boogiemonsters took the stage. Sean and Ivor danced and took turns with Vex and Mondo on the microphones. Much more comfortable with his rhyming ability now that he and Ivor had honed their skills, Sean felt natural with his lips against the mic, chanting reggae style for the crowd. Though partially blinded by the bright lights in his eyes, Sean could see Lauryn Hill smiling and nodding her head to the beat. Charged by the approval he saw in her face, Sean finished out the rhyme with energy.

When the performance was over and Sean stepped down off the stage, he was immediately greeted by Lauryn Hill. "Hey, I'm Lauryn," she said, smiling at him.

"I know." Sean nodded and smiled back as he put out his hand.

"You were the one that was chanting, right?" Lauryn asked.

"Yeah," Sean said. "It's my thing—it's what I do."

"I love it," Lauryn said. "Even though I'm a hip-hop artist, I love reggae. What you did tonight was fresh. Hey, I have an idea," she continued, "why don't you guys come sit at our table for the rest of the performances? I'd love to talk to you some more."

Sean was thrilled to be sitting across the table from the Fugees, and by the end of the evening, he found that he and Lauryn Hill had quite a bit in common—including their love of reggae, a dislike for gansta rap, and a love for hip-hop with an uptown New York feel to it. They had spent only one evening together, and already they seemed like old friends.

But in addition to the friends they were making in the music business, Sean and the others continued to hang out with D. Ever amazed at his knowledge of the Bible, the Boogiemonsters often invited him over to study with them.

"All right, I have to know," Sean said one night as they all sat around with their Bibles open. "The mark of the beast. What is it, really? Does the Bible tell us what it is, or is it all just a weird mystery we're never supposed to understand?"

"We're supposed to understand it," D assured him. "In fact, if you let it, the Bible interprets itself. The apocalyptic books make more sense if you read them together, because they help to explain each other. And one of the prophetic books that helps to fill in the puzzle pieces in Revelation is the book of Daniel. Before we talk about the mark of the beast, let's find out who the beast is."

Sean and the others listened eagerly as D spoke.

"Daniel 7 tells us that in prophecy, beasts represent kingdoms or powers," D said. "The Bible gives us clues so that we can identify through history which powers are represented by which beasts."

"Like what?" Ivor questioned.

"Well, like the third beast in Daniel 7," D pointed out. "We know that it represents Greece because of when it comes on the scene—right after the

Babylonian Empire and the Medo-Persian Empire."

"Why does it have wings?" Sean wondered.

"Wings represent speed," D answered. "The four wings on the beast represent the speed with which Alexander the Great conquered the known world."

"What about the four heads?" Vex asked.

"Well," D continued, "the beast has four heads because Alexander the Great died, and his empire was divided between his four generals. The beasts in Daniel are the same beasts as in Revelation. This helps us figure out what power the beast with the mark represents. The number 666 helps us pinpoint it. It's amazing. All you have to do is know your history and follow the timeline, and you can figure it out."

"I knew it had nothing to do with the symbol on a box of laundry soap." Sean elbowed Ivor in the ribs and both of them chuckled as they remembered their trip to the basement as kids. "So much for our cousin Susan's theory."

As D talked, the mysteries began to unfold, and Sean soaked up every word. When D pointed out the Scripture verses that gave them important clues to how to understand the strange symbols in prophecy, Sean felt his brain was being stretched like a rubber band.

"I can't get enough of this. I finally understand it. How do you know all this stuff?" Sean asked, shaking his head.

D shrugged. "I learned it at church."

Ivor looked determined. "I want to go to your church."

D seemed a little uncomfortable. "Well, I haven't really been to my church in a long time. Right now

I don't really practice what my church teaches."

"What difference does it make?" Ivor persisted. "You can still go, can't you? Will you take us to your church on Sabbath? Saturday?"

After some convincing, D promised he would, and the next Saturday morning the Boogiemonsters went to church.

CHAPTER 12

T his is crazy," Ivor said to Sean. "I'm learning so much, and it's so fascinating. Sometimes I think I'm more interested in this than being famous."

Sean nodded. "I know what you mean."

"I don't even want to smoke marijuana anymore," Ivor continued, amazed at his own words. "I mean, the Holy Spirit gives us wisdom, right? And our bodies are like temples for the Holy Spirit. And smoking marijuana damages that temple. Sean, I'm never going to light another joint. Ever."

Sean, Ivor, Vex, and Mondo all decided that they wanted to be baptized again—this time knowing what they believed and understanding why they were being baptized.

Not coincidentally, after being baptized underwater, the Boogiemonsters decided to name their first recording *Riders of the Storm: the Underwater Album*. Excited about their faith, the Boogiemonsters were anxious to share through the music what they had learned.

On the night of their album release party the Boogiemonsters waited backstage with their microphones while being introduced to the hyped crowd. "Can you believe this is really happening?" Sean whispered to his brother.

"That's Red Alert out there introducing us," Ivor said in disbelief.

"Some of the famous artists we've listened to are now out there in the audience, here to listen to us," Mondo added. "To *us*," he repeated emphatically.

Ivor smiled as Red Alert announced the Boogiemonsters. "This is it!" he whispered. "Time for the Boogiemonsters to deliver the three angels' messages!"

"They're not even going to know what hit them," Vex said. "We're like sheep in wolves' clothing. We may look like the world and sound like the world, but that's just to get the world's attention for God."

Red and blue lights swirled the stage, and Indian chant music poured from the speakers onto the shrieking crowd. Still standing backstage out of sight, the Boogiemonsters lifted their microphones to their lips and began to speak in unison.

"Our Father, which art in heaven, hallowed is your name. . . . "

As the sound of four voices speaking the Lord's Prayer filled the club the alcohol and marijuana-driven crowd responded in a roar of enthusiasm. When the show was over Derrick dragged them around the room, introducing them to the big names in the industry.

"That was the best show I have ever seen. I'm serious," a man with a familiar face said when Derrick introduced them. "Really incredible. The best."

"Who was that?" Sean asked when the man left. "He looks familiar."

"He's the manager for another band!" Derrick

said, grinning and shaking his head.

"He manages another band, and he just said our show is the best he's ever seen?" Sean asked in disbelief.

"Yo, that was tight tonight. Get used to the compliments." Derrick barely paused before introducing them to another enthusiastic guest.

"I've never been so pumped," Sean sighed when the evening ended and they waved goodbye to fans through the limousine windows.

"I know—out there tonight, we were rubbing shoulders with people we've idolized," Ivor added. "And now they're listening to us." They leaned back in the soft leather seats, exhausted. It was late. They'd given all their energy to the performance and then even more to talking with their fans.

"You guys ever listen to Biggie Smalls?" Derrick asked, leaning against the seat with his eyes closed.

"Are you kidding?" Sean said. "Of course we do. He's one of the best."

"Good. Glad you like him. Because you're touring with him in a couple of weeks."

The Boogiemonsters' mouths dropped open. It was a whole new world for all of them, and the surprises just kept getting better.

"This rap, hip-hop, reggae gospel thing you've got going is really stirring up the attention," Derrick told them. "It's great. You guys have the magic to take us all to the top with you."

Sean closed his eyes. Images from the evening floated and crossed in his mind. Although he couldn't put his finger on it, something about the whole experience bothered him. "Do you think it's weird," he confided in Ivor one day, "that Derrick admits he's an atheist, and Francesca practices witchcraft and paganism—belief systems that are basically anti-God—and yet neither of them seem to mind our spirituality?"

"I know what you mean," Ivor responded. "You know, Fran told us she worships the universe. On our album cover where we all gave thanks to God she used her space to give thanks to the universe. It's strange how light and darkness seem to be working together in harmony in our work."

"Exactly." Sean nodded. "I have this feeling about it, like something's wrong."

The Boogiemonsters were making quite an impression on both their fans and the reporters who interviewed them. People in the music scene were surprised to see four guys who talked non-stop about God show up in the studio with their hair in dreadlocks, wearing expensive nose rings and earrings and on-the-edge fashions.

"Our goal is to reach the hip-hop generation for God," they told the interviewers. "Like sheep in wolves' clothing."

The idea of sheep in wolves' clothing seemed to follow them, and the Boogiemonsters enjoyed the shock effect. Their fans and promoters alike embraced their conflicted image. And appearances on MTV, BET and Soul Train gave them an opportunity to share what they knew about God with a wide audience.

★ ★ ★

Sean yawned and looked out the window of the

studio. Below, the lights of Times Square sparkled and danced in the darkness. The Boogiemonsters had been in the studio all night making music. Now came the down time, when the group hung out together while the engineer mixed what they had recorded. Often, during these times of waiting, the friends would study together, exploring the prophecies about the second coming of Jesus and the time of trouble that would precede that event. They could see when they watched the news and saw world events that some of the very things the Bible had predicted were happening, and it made them all even more excited to get the word out.

"Man, this thing is really going to happen." Mondo emphasized his words by tapping lightly on his Bible.

"Yeah," Sean said pensively, "but do you ever feel like something's not right? Look at our lifestyle. Look at how we talk and act. Our words say, 'Look at Jesus.' But everything else about us says 'Look at the Boogiemonsters.' You know what I mean?"

"The thing is," Vex countered, "you can't be a humble rap star. There's no such thing. We have to brag about ourselves. It's part of the culture."

"But can you imagine Jesus standing on a stage bragging about Himself?" Ivor wondered aloud.

"Then what are we doing here, man?" Mondo shook his head, his face scrunched with conflicting emotions.

Lounging in the studio, watching the city lights fade into the brightness of the sunrise, the friends pondered the dilemma, each lost in private thoughts.

The days passed and life went on an usual. "Hey, more fan mail," Vex called as he walked in from outside and spilled a pile of letters on the table.

Each of the guys wandered in, sat down, and picked up a piece of mail to read. They still got a kick out of fan mail.

Sean read from a flowered sheet, laughed, and tossed it aside. "Another marriage proposal," he said. "Any takers?"

Everyone laughed, and Mondo ripped one of the letters open to read it. "'You guys are so deep. Your lyrics and music really make me think.'"

"Cool," Ivor said. "Here's another one. This one's nice. "'My son loves your music.'"

Vex seemed to be trapped in his own little world as he scanned the letter he held in his hand. "Wait, listen to this one," he said, finally looking up. Something about his tone stopped the others and they all gave him their attention.

"'Dear Boogiemonsters, I am a great fan of yours and I appreciate your music,'" Vex began. "'You are doing a great work for the hip-hop community. However, I have a question. You guys say that you are a rap group for God. The Bible says in Amos 3:3, "Can two walk together, except they be agreed?" And 2 Corinthians 6:14 says, "for what fellowship hath righteousness with unrighteousness? and what communion hath light with darkness?"'"

Vex stopped and looked up. "Want to hear more?" he asked.

They nodded. Sean shrugged. "Yeah, sure."

With a deep breath Vex continued. "'The Bible

also points out that we should "abstain from all appearance of evil." That's in 1 Thessalonians 5:22. In light of these scriptural truths, how can you have a name like Boogiemonsters, and yet profess to serve God?'"

The three young men looked at Vex in surprise.

"That's it?"

"Yeah."

"Well, that was unexpected," Sean said finally. "Sounds like that guy is a little off the deep end."

"He's crazy," Mondo agreed. "A religious nut."

"Fruit loops," Ivor concurred.

But that night after Sean went to bed, the words of the letter continued to play over and over in his head. Sure, they had all dismissed the writer as a crazy fan. But something about what he said made sense. It actually echoed some of the concerns Sean had been feeling about the direction of the group.

Sean took a deep breath and closed his eyes. But no matter how hard he tried, he couldn't get to sleep.

CHAPTER 13

The next morning when Sean stumbled into the kitchen for breakfast he noticed that Ivor, Mondo, and Vex all looked exhausted.

"You guys didn't sleep either?" Sean asked, pouring a glass of milk.

"Nope." Ivor opened his mouth in a cavernous yawn as he rubbed his eyes. "Man, all I could think about was that fan letter. It wouldn't let me go. Maybe the dude has a point."

Sean took a sip of milk and put the glass down on the counter. "You know, I've been thinking. When I was a kid I was fascinated with monsters because they were evil. Now that I'm a Christian, calling myself a 'monster' seems so opposite of what I want."

"Maybe we should change our name," Vex suggested. "We called our first album *Riders of the Storm*. That name fits us better as Christians than Boogiemonsters. What do you guys think?"

The idea was passed in unanimous agreement. After a strange letter and a sleepless night, the Boogiemonsters had decided to change their name to reflect a new direction. In name and in deed, they would be Riders of the Storm. All they had to do was convince the record label.

"No." The word seemed to land with a thud on

the president's desk, and Sean, Ivor, Vex, and Mondo stared at the record company president in surprise. Their request to change their name from Boogiemonsters to Riders of the Storm was dismissed in a single syllable.

The president cleared his throat and looked at them matter-of-factly. "We've spent a fortune building an image around the name Boogiemonsters. The name's unique. It sticks. Changing your name in the middle of everything is bad for business. Sorry, but you *are* the Boogiemonsters."

The friends left the office feeling deflated. But they understood. They just hadn't thought of it that way before.

"OK, guys," Derrick looked down at his notes and twirled a pencil between his thumb and index finger. "Here's what your schedule looks like this week. Monday, you're in Michigan, signing autographs at a music store. Tuesday you have an interview with a staff writer from a magazine. Who wants to take it? Mondo? Sean?"

"I did the last one," Mondo complained.

"I did it twice in a row," Sean reminded him.

"Don't even look at me," Ivor said.

"Vex, it's yours. Thanks, buddy," Derrick continued, scribbling on his notepad. "OK, let's see. Wednesday—big promotional thing in Texas. Need everybody there. Thursday, you're all flying to California. Friday night you have three radio interviews and a performance in Los Angeles. Oh, and be careful who you hang out with while you're there. We've had some issues with the whole East Coast rap versus West Coast rap. It seems there are guys who will invite you to go party with them, but it's actually a setup to get you off by yourselves. They'll have guys waiting to jump you. Just keep your eyes open and use your heads. Any questions?"

"I think we've got it," Ivor nodded.

"I'm going to need a brace for my hand after doing so many signings." Mondo massaged his right wrist in preparation. "Especially if fans are lined up around the block to meet us like they were in Chicago."

The other guys laughed. In the beginning, all of the interviews, autographs, video shoots, and nights spent in the recording studio were exciting and fun. But as time went on, it started to feel like what it actually was: work.

All week Ivor seemed disquieted by his thoughts, and Friday afternoon in California he brought up some concerns to the group. "You know, all of us have come to an understanding that Saturday is God's Sabbath. We've found out that Sabbath is supposed to be a day that we celebrate the fact that God has revealed Himself through His creation. And to celebrate the fact that He's re-creating us to be like Him."

"Yeah?" Sean looked at Ivor quizzically. "What are you trying to say?"

"Well," Ivor continued. "When Sabbath starts on Friday night at sundown, we're usually performing in a club where people are drinking and mellowing out with marijuana—stuff we don't do anymore. Saturdays we spend doing interviews and autographing records and stuff. Sure, we know what day it is, but I feel like we're not honoring it the way it was meant to be honored."

"That's been bothering me, too," Mondo said.

"But our biggest venues are on Sabbath. Every single weekend. Do you think God really wants us to stop performing on Sabbath?"

"What if we just ask Him?" Sean proposed. "We could just lay it before Him and ask for a sign, and let Him tell us."

"That's actually not a bad idea," Ivor spoke up. "Let's see, it's Friday. And we have three radio interviews and a performance tonight. Let's ask God to cancel those appointments if He doesn't want us to perform on Sabbath anymore. What do you think?"

"It's a rare thing for us to even get one cancellation, much less four," Vex noted. "Four cancellations would be unheard of."

"Then it would definitely be a sign," Mondo said. "Let's pray about it."

With their friends and road managers gathered around, Ivor led them in prayer. "Lord, if you do not want us to perform on Sabbath anymore, please cancel all four appointments tonight. Amen."

The guys look at each other and took a breath. They felt certain that in a matter of hours God would make His will known. The thought was exciting. Even so there was a lot to do to get ready for the evening and their first appointment.

The limousine pulled up to the curb next to the radio station, and the Boogiemonsters and their entourage stepped out.

"Here we are," Mondo breathed.

They stood on the sidewalk, ready to go inside. They'd prayed. Their future was in God's hands. What would happen now?

The radio representative came out, wringing his hands apologetically. "Guys, I'm sorry. Something has happened. There won't be an interview tonight."

"No way!" Ivor had the same look on his face as everyone else. Amazement.

"What are the odds of that happening?" Vex asked as they climbed back into the limo. "Is God giving us the answer?"

"We prayed that all *four* appointments would be canceled," Sean reminded him. "Let's wait and see what happens."

When they arrived at the second radio station, again someone met them at the door with an apology. The interview had been canceled.

This time the entire entourage was silent as they traveled to their third radio interview. There seemed to be intensity in the air as all of them waited curiously to see what would happen next. Vex got out of the limo. The others waited.

No one told them the interview was cancelled.

For no one came out of the radio station studio at all.

Vex knocked on the closed door. It was locked.

At the third radio station, no one was there.

Dumbfounded, the Boogiemonsters, their friends and road managers took in the significance of the third unfulfilled engagement.

"This is unbelievable." Sean stared through the darkened window of the limousine, looking up at the skyscrapers around them. One appointment remained—the live club performance. None of their performances had ever been cancelled before.

The Boogiemonsters arrived at the club expecting screaming fans and camera flashes, but all was dark and silent. Apparently, just prior to their arrival the fire marshal had shut down the club, and the show had been called off. Their fourth cancellation signaled the end of the evening for the Boogiemonsters. Sean, Ivor, Vex and Mondo looked at each other knowingly.

"This is God's answer," Sean said, shaking his head in disbelief. Excitement filled him as he thought about God's powerful response to their prayers, and he could tell by the looks on the other guys' faces that they were just as impressed.

"Well," Ivor said with a smile. "We've got God's answer. I just wonder what the label's answer is going to be when we tell them we don't want to perform on Sabbath anymore."

"Noble aspirations, guys. Really." The president of the record company didn't seem very impressed. "But the fact is, you signed a contract that requires you to perform in a certain manner. Your biggest performances happen on Friday nights, and that is what you will do. If you try to get out of it, that's considered a breach of contract, and I will take you to court. Are we clear?"

After their meeting with the president, Derrick took them aside. "OK, guys, what's going on here?" he asked. Concern filled his face. "I sympathize with you about your whole Sabbath thing. I really do. But you're messing up here. There's already been talk around the record label that you guys are starting to sound too preachy."

Disenchanted, Sean realized that something was changing. *How much can I do for God while Satan is calling all the shots?* he wondered. *The label will let us live for God only as long as it makes them money.*

"Something strange is happening," Ivor confessed to Sean one morning. "I feel like I'm getting a message from God."

"What is He saying?" Sean asked, knowing the answer in his heart already.

"I hear Him saying, 'Soon your career as a hip-hop artist will be over.'"

Vex walked into the room, a look of awe on his face. "Guys," he said. "I just had a dream that was so *real*. I saw and felt this explosion of fire. Rising out of the flames, unscathed, were the four of us. Each one of us was raising a hand in the air. And in each of our raised hands was a microphone."

"What an impressive dream," Ivor said. "I wonder what it means."

It was a dream that would continue to intrigue all of them.

CHAPTER 14

Strange things began to happen in Sean's mind. The entertainment he used to love seemed empty all of a sudden. Everything they had devoted themselves to—the monsters, the martial arts, the music—it was all a substitute for something more powerful and more amazing. Sean began to realize that everything he had wanted, he had been given. But now he was ready to let it go. He wondered how his brother would react to the news.

"I was at the club in Philadelphia the other night after we performed," Ivor recounted to Sean during one of their conversations. "You know, just to mingle and hang out with fans. But something happened that really freaked me out. It was like God opened my eyes so that I could see the evil in that room. I could almost see the evil spirits controlling the bodies of the people who were on the dance floor, and I just wanted to leave."

"Remember how I used to dream about the day when I'd be old enough to go to the clubs?" Sean said. "Now I don't want to be there."

"Sean, I don't know how you are going to take this," Ivor confessed. "But I can't do this anymore. I can't be as close to God as I want to be and still be in this business."

Sean blinked. "Are you kidding?"

Ivor shook his head. "I know it sounds sudden and everything, but—"

"No, no, no," Sean interrupted. "It's just that I came to the same conclusion. I can't do it anymore either. I want to work for God, not a record label."

The brothers smiled at each other.

But one thing stood between them and freedom, and it was big. They were bound to an eight-album recording contract with Pendulum/EMI Records.

"Man, when I think of all the times God has showed up in our lives, even when we were kids and didn't know anything about Him," Sean said. "And that Friday night He canceled all four of our gigs to answer our prayers. I know if we pray about this, God will handle it."

Sean and Ivor prayed together, and then waited to see what God would do. It didn't take long. A few days later, the Boogiemonsters received a phone call from their manager, Derrick.

"I don't know how to tell you this, guys," Derrick said. "But Pendulum/EMI Records has folded. I'm sorry, but the bottom line is you no longer have a recording contract. You're on your own."

Sean and Ivor whooped and slapped a high-five as they celebrated the news. "Are you kidding? Are you kidding?" Sean kept asking.

For Sean, the celebration was short-lived. He stood on Aunt Faye's porch with Ivor, looking at Mondo and Vex in confusion. "What do you mean, you're going back to the industry? The two of you are going to try to get another contract?" he asked. "How can you give up the freedom that God just gave us?"

The four of them stood on Aunt Faye's doorstep, at a junction in their careers and in their friendships.

Mondo looked down at his feet, and then back up at Sean and Ivor. "Guys, we've got to do our thing."

"I guess you already know that Sean and I aren't going with you," Ivor said. "We feel like God is calling us to do something else."

"Yeah, we figured. Looks like we're all headed in different directions," Vex mused softly.

Sean felt like a part of him was dying. He looked at Vex and Mondo and thought about everything they had been through together during the last few years. There was so much he wanted to say, but it all stayed in his heart, heavy and unspoken.

Mondo stuck out his hand. "All friends to the end?" he said with a catch in his voice.

Each of the others put their hands on his. Ivor offered a prayer. It was the last time they prayed together as the Boogiemonsters.

★ ★ ★

"Are we crazy?" Ivor looked down at his new Target store uniform almost in disbelief. It had been a few weeks since Vex and Mondo went back to New York, and Sean and Ivor moved back in with their parents in Virginia. "Can you believe what we just gave up?"

Sean laughed. "Yeah, but we've got our lives back. Now we can do whatever it is God wants us to do. And for now it looks like God wants you to work at Target."

To Sean, the news of Biggie Smalls' murder came as a brutal reminder of the life they had left behind. Sean knew that if they had stayed in the music industry, it would have been impossible to avoid being sucked up into the tornado of rivalry that kept East Coast and West Coast rappers at odds—only a matter of time before they would have been unwilling participants in a war that wasn't theirs.

"Remember Vex's dream?" Sean asked after they watched the news report on Biggie Smalls' death. "We really did come out of the fire unscathed."

"Yes, we did. Thank God," Ivor said sincerely. "The weird thing is, in Vex's dream, when we came out of the fire, we were each still holding microphones. What do you suppose that meant?"

Sean shrugged. "I guess we'll just have to wait and see."

EPILOGUE

Sean **Myers** is currently youth pastor of a church in Georgia. As Vex's dream predicted, Sean is back at the microphone for God. His mission is to reach generations of kids with the message of the gospel through his story.

In 2005, he picked up a magazine in a grocery store with a picture of popular rap artist 50 Cent on the front cover. In the middle of the magazine was a picture of the Boogiemonsters on a milk carton with the caption, "Boogiemonsters—where are they?" As the memories came flooding back, Sean praised God for leading him in an exciting new direction, and for the new life he enjoys with his wife, Veronica.

Ivor **Myers** is now the pastor of a church in California. Every week he finds himself at the microphone speaking the truths to his church members that God has revealed to him . Even though he was teased for his accent as a child and developed a fear of speaking, he never has that fear when talking about God. He also makes regular appearances on 3ABN, a television broadcasting network dedicated to the spread of the gospel. He enjoys sharing his story around the world, and recently wrote a book on his experiences. He and his wife, Atonte, have four children.